Praise for **Daddy Show**

In this blazing collection, Bakar Wilson dives headfirst into the raw edges of identity, love, faith, and worship—to 'navigate the body like an elegant puzzle.' This poetry offers a lyric typology of desire—it howls, whispers, laments, and roars. At turns fierce and searching, piercing and attentive, *Daddy Show* is a dare, a fever dream, a change-agent, a psalm rippling with cadenced grace and incinerating power. A true gift and essential voice in queer liberation.

> —**Margot Douaihy**, *USA Today* bestselling author of *Scorched Grace* and *Blessed Water* (Gillian Flynn Books, 2024 and 2023)

Bakar Wilson's gift as a poet is to stamp his experience with wit and humor. As the reincarnation of Lot's wife, he can claim, "This time I'm prepared to live," and we need not take it with a grain of salt. And in a spoof of the personal ad, he advises, "If interested, reply to men / you see on the streets." Wilson walks through the streets of these poems as a person and poet you would be happy to know. His poetry has all the honest ambiguity and endurance of survivorship.

> —**Mark Jarman**, is the award winning author of fifteen books, most recently *Zeno's Eternity* (Paul Dry Books, 2023), *The Heronry* (Sarabande Books, 2017), and *Bone Fires: New and Selected Poems* (Sarabande Books, 2011)

Bakar Wilson speaks difficult truths in lucid, terse lines. *Daddy Show* demonstrates courage, wisdom, and a keen ear for the drama to be found in reticence. I admire the patient attentiveness behind these direct yet gnomic poems, their narratives sharpened by audacity and a tragicomic showmanship, a knowledge of how to create a riveting, emotionally turbulent spectacle.

> —**Wayne Koestenbaum**, is author of nineteen books, most recently *Stubble Archipelago* (MIT Press, 2024), *Ultramarine* (Nightboat Books, 2022) and *The Cheerful Scapegoat: Fables* (MIT Press, 2021)

Bakar Wilson's exciting and expertly drawn *Daddy Show* reveals many complex paths, embedded in the book's self-reflexive query: "Are you good at mazes?" Wilson, in fact, is perfect at mazes, offering the making and landscape of the mind's interior, moving between the psyche and pulsing city moored to the memory of the speaker's "father, a void… without a word to anchor his soul," through Wilson's "New York City, there is always light Showing you the way. The terrain/ Is different but no less diabolical./You traverse. It trips…" Here, Wilson offers a brilliant alchemy that "…stings the tongue too tough/ and drains every ounce of moisture/ out of me until I'm nothing but mineral./ This time I'm ready/ excited about the things that await me." If this is a book of complex celebrations, it is also an account of riveting alliances and ethical ascents, ever steady in the face of critique: "He's engaged."/"What are you doing?"/"This is wrong."/ My stock answer of course,/ "Well, if it's not me, it's going to be someone else." /And then I'm absolved./ We reach the roof." Building into the winding flights of erotic enactments, Wilson's *Daddy Show* secures precise routes between respite and reflection, "…How far do I cast?/ Well, you can't afford /this shade, actually, I'm/too stark for you, too much minimalist, too much/Mensa." Wilson's fierce erudition is tender, fun, and deeply moving, a gorgeous debut that travels effortlessly between wonder and reclamation.

> **—Ronaldo V. Wilson**, is the award winning author of *Lucy 72* (1913 Press, 2018), *Farther Traveler: Poetry, Prose, Other* (Counterpath Press, 2015), *Poems of the Black Object* (Futurepoem Books, 2009), and *Narrative of the Life of the Brown Boy and the White Man* (University of Pittsburgh, 2008)

Daddy Show

by Bakar Wilson

Copyright © 2025 by Bakar Wilson

All rights reserved. No part of this book may be reproduced in any manner without written consent except for the quotation of short passages used inside of an article, criticism, or review.

Get Fresh Publishing, A Non-Profit Corp.
PO Box 901
Union, NJ 07083

www.gfbpublishing.org

ISBN: 9798218623302
Library of Congress Control Number: 2025933604

This book was typeset in Avenir and Pincoyablack

Cover art by Krista Franklin
Interior by Anny Caba | AnnyCaba.com
Author photo by Gabriel García Román for his Queer Icons series

For

Shelia Ann Wilson
&
Jerry Wayne Wilson, Sr.

Contents

I — 1

Poet/Manifesto	2
Landscape	3
For Mom	4
My Father's Shoes	5
The Fight	7
Levitation	8
Portrait	9
Door-to-Door	10
Possum Feet	11
In Christ, Drowning	12
Reincarnated as Lot's Wife Again and Again	13
Repent for Your Sins or Burn Forever in a Pit of Hellfire and Brimstone	14
Heartbreaker	15
The Games You Played	16
Through the Window	17
Letters	18
Mother	24

II — 25

What Are You Doing?	26
Remembering Samantha Fox	27

Manhattan	28
Three Wishes	29
Three Wishes II	30
Anti-War Haiku	31
S/M	32
Clothes/Whore	33
Fucking DJ	34
City Streets	36
On Seeing Richter	38
Whore/Genius	39

III   41

Love Poem #3	42
Grindr Vibin'	43
Sizing Him Up	44
Same-Sex Coupling	45
Destruction/Desire	46
I Go Around Collecting Men	47
Consent	48
love poem #9	49
I Should Have Been a Gay Porn Star	50
J/K	51
American Logic	52
Love Poem #15	53
The Milky Way	54
Appreciation	55

I

Poet/Manifesto

I am not a/part of your admin

I do not/in your God

Me pulling at levers anyway
thinking that it may make a difference

I want nothing to do with your fuck market

I

I

S/he is a citizen/a ruling despot

When you stop killing people who look/fuck like me

This country is a fucking/I abstain

American/a concept sold to everyone so only a few prosper

I intend to queer

Your ink/a pall

A ~~jezebel~~ rent/boy is plotting our ultimate demise

Landscape

I promise I'll be good in this terrain.
There are men in corners, but
I know how to navigate things.
It's beautiful here though:
mountains cut like teeth,
they scrape this sky.
I'm pulsing in the valley
trying to figure out
what these jams are made of.
Raucous beats dreaming about
drama in the dark.

In New York City, there is always light
showing you the way. The terrain
is different but no less diabolical.
You traverse. It trips.
The beats are different too.
They pulsate more bass.
Shred the body's flesh without a bomb.

For Mom

Rose petals purse
Linger on stems
Pass days patiently
Until exploding into
Blossom
She appears
Lauds the bright red
Splotches on the ends
Of thorned stems
She loves thorns
Those are her favorite
Parts of the bush
They protect the soft
Silk of the flower petal
Gloves protect her hands
From her favorite thorns
She takes out her shears
And begins to cut

My Father's Shoes

There is a nervous silence in the house
as I walk into my parents' bedroom:
the cold, aching hardwood floor
creaks under my bare feet as I enter
the one room I do not belong to.
My palms sweat
as the excitement of getting caught
moves through my body like the
blood in my veins,
causing me to slightly hesitate.
I ignore my mother's things,
this time,
and walk to my father's jewelry box
that sits on top of his chest of drawers,
which is slightly taller than I am.
I stand on the tips of my toes,
reach for the box,
and pull out old rings, an old wristwatch.
I put them on
as if transposing manhood onto me.

*I am a man
in an eight-year-old body.*

I notice a pair of my father's shoes,
and I try them on
to see how much further I have to go.
I clop around the bedroom
as my toes do little tricks
that keep the shoes from dropping
to the floor.

"I am a man now," I think to myself
as I walk around the room
in my father's shoes,
trying not to fall.

The Fight

Her song   is a needle piercing skin
His is ashamed
Her song blocks out the sun   leaving only shadows
His song creeps   cautiously through hers
This time he means it when he says   he's sorry
Strums her pain like a guitar
My brother and I listen closely for songs
Our father whispers words that guarantee forgiveness
Sometimes she believes him
Other times   she erupts
Clouding each room with smoke and soot
Today her face is slick with tears
Her song   scatters itself throughout our house
He has no song
My father has been unfaithful again

Levitation
    for Nikky Finney

Tossing and turning on air,
a voice moves over my flesh
like water, and I know I am
not right. I fall to my bed
on top of unruly sheets, waking,
screaming because I did not touch
the high corners of my room,
the moon, or walk on the roof.
What kind of a dream is this?
Baritone voice preaching to me
like God. Words ringing in my
ears like bells as I wake on my
bed, still bouncing from the impact.
Mama runs in, asking questions
I do not have the answers to.
She says everything will be okay,
rubs my head, holds me as if
I was breathing my last breath.
I want to know the secret.
I want to go back to that
moment. Little body floating,
darkness, sleep. I want to know
what was lifting me out of my bed.

Portrait

This Barkley L. Hendricks piece
reminds me of my father.
The manicured beard,
the sunglasses,
toothpick firmly hanging out of
his mouth. He seems so cool.
The resemblance is spooky.
I want to talk to it,
ask the portrait what it
feels like to look like my father,
and yet to have never known him.
Then I remember.
I wish my fingertips could touch
the palette, perhaps read the
brushstrokes for answers,
or maybe ask the questions
my mouth cannot utter.
But all I do is stand, stare,
and think of him,
my father,
who only lives in photos.

Door-to-Door

In a suit, I went door-to-door,
the steaming hot sun staring at me
like God's golden eye. Knocking on doors,
I gave witness to all his fine works,
quoted Bible verses, made Jesus my lover.
Sometimes, my mother was with me;
other times, she was at home,
pleasing the father in other ways.
Out in the streets, I was spreading his word,
making him proud of me.
I sat on plush couches in nice houses,
a little Black boy in White people's homes,
telling them about Jehovah, about the paradise Earth
his followers would inherit.

My father, a void, hangs over me now,
without a word to anchor his soul.

Possum Feet
> *for Misty*

The little girl with plaits
Sprouting out the top
Of her head
Would dance
I watched her playfully
Laughed at her flapping arms
Her pogo-stick legs
As she hopped
Around her grandmother's
Juke joint
A mini shotgun
Painted dirty white
With rusted red bars
On the windows
Juke box in the corner
Shooting out
Blues jazz disco
She would dance barefoot
On the hardwood floor
Polished with ebony black oil
Grandma dubbed her
"Possum feet"
And she would dance
Until the bottoms of her feet
Matched the floor

In Christ, Drowning

The full moon coaxes waves from
the ocean on a night when the wind
moves through you like a miracle.
You stand alone, teasing the tide
with bare feet. You are afraid
of the water, of being alone,
of the life you lead.
Tenderly, your foot tests the water.
Colder than you imagine, you pull back.
You want to go out there. You wish
to walk on water, like Jesus, if
the Bible story is really true.
Lucky Jesus, able to go from continent
to continent on his own two feet. When
he was tired, he probably just sat for a while
on the ocean. He would play with the
dolphins, or the fish.
Sharks wouldn't attack him, because he's
Jesus, and surely the sharks did not want
to go to hell for eating God's son. He'd get
up after his rest and continue on his way.
You are not Jesus, but there is something
attractive about that water. The grace of
the waves lulls you into balance. You still
want to go out there, and even though
you are not Jesus, you run out and baptize
yourself in the cold, unclean salt water.

Reincarnated as Lot's Wife Again and Again

I've gotten good at not looking back.
Behind me the world is ablaze.
I can feel the heat of fire rain
on my spine,
but I finally don't care.
I'm going to miss my old lives.
They were times of abundant pleasure
even though all around me
things were slowly crumbling into dust.
I'm finally tired of it,
and I'm tired of salt.
It stings the tongue too tough
and drains every ounce of moisture
out of me until I'm nothing but mineral.
This time I'm ready,
excited about the things that await me.
This time I'm prepared to live.

Repent for Your Sins or Burn Forever in a Pit of Hellfire and Brimstone

The man holds a sign on the sidewalk,
claiming that he knows God's intentions.
How arrogant,
to think one knows God's intentions,
and to have the audacity to brag about it
to other people he does not know.
So haughty:
"Repent for your sins."
To repent for my sins
would be like having a second job.
I would be constantly repenting
for shit every day
for a few hours, probably.
Who has the time?

And as far as this pit is concerned,
does it even really exist? If God is a
loving and a forgiving God, and a
gracious God, why would he make
people who curse or have sex out of
wedlock, or drink to excess, or do drugs
burn in a place forever? Isn't that a bit much?
Murder only gets you 25 to life in some states,
and life ends eventually.
Forever is a long time to burn for a poor
sense of judgment,
a long time to burn
for compulsions one cannot control.

Heartbreaker

The tent at the fair
Holds hands on a day
That whispers autumn

Inside/internalized
Holly's mother tells
Me my right hand breaks hearts
Holds intervals of longing

Shy children don't know
That lust gluts wringing hands
And muddy rivers cover tracks

He didn't even know I was there

The Games You Played

He is a man asleep on a couch.
You are merely a boy
whose curiosity and disdain
have left you scorched.
Socked feet skate on the hardwood
floor in the living room.
You wonder if he is really asleep as
you slip your hand beneath
boxer shorts. His dick is already hard.
The cat, a witness, turns his head from
the TV blaring an infomercial selling
something. You know the cat doesn't
know what's going on, but you can't
help but wonder. He stares nonplussed as
if he knows the repercussions.
What happens next will run you
like an engine runs a car into a ditch,
or off a cliff.

Through the Window

I am watching you walk
across the backyard
wearing those
shorts I like, snug in
all the right places.
From the kitchen, my eyes
peruse, snatch visual pictures
of you to use later.

Other me is watching me
from the dining room.
Summer sunlight slides
through windowpanes.
It is midafternoon,
my stomach queasy
seeing my own desire.
You are not mine, nor
do I really want you, the
actual person; I really just
want the shell, the body
to play with, experiment,
figure myself out.

You are a step-man,
married to my mom.
I am a boy who sits
in the Kingdom Hall,
split in two on Sunday
mornings and Thursday
nights. My kind, a virus
that threatens to invade.

Our mouths go dry
as we watch you
walk down the hill.

Letters

i.

It's OK, Daddy; I understand now.
I get that you were a Black Man
in a small country town in west
Tennessee. I know the anger
you had losing your father, shot
by a man who was your mother's
sidepiece, while he was away at war.
When he came back and found out,
you would become fatherless,
like me now.

ii.

I'm sure it was hard to get work, despite
your college degree in drafting.
General Electric was always passing
you up when it was time for promotion.
It's fine. I know how quickly things turn around.
I remember you out in the streets. You were
hardly ever home. J remembers you, barely.
I can see how you, a Man with so much, yet
so little, would just do things your way,
becoming the third largest drug dealer in west Tennessee.
It's OK. You were always the Man. Everyone loved
you, always. I remember once, at Grandma's beer
joint, I shot my mouth off at one of her regulars.
I was displeased. She snatched my arm so quick.
"You need to be more like your daddy. He's
cool with everyone. Everyone loves him."
I never forgot that; you have to be nice to people,
even if you don't like them, a realization difficult for
this child to swallow.

iii.

I was so scared of you. My mind unable to
reconcile how you were so loved, yet so mean to me.
I get it. You were trying to make me tough,
your sissy little boy. I remember you yelling
at me because I was walking around the house
with a limp wrist, mimicking Mama. Boys
don't do that; only girls do. Or the time you bought me
the baseball glove, and we played catch in the backyard.
It was fine, at first, but then, as I backed away, short
baseball tosses turned. You tossed it far and high in the air
and the ball hit me on my right ear, hard.
I began to cry. You were furious,
threatening to give me something to cry about.
It's OK, Daddy, I understand now.
You wanted me to be a Man,
to walk around with your swagger,
knowing that no one is going to fuck
with you. That's how I am now,
except, sometimes I get fucked by men.
This is what I have crunched
in my mind for years. Would you have still loved me?
Would you have still loved your little boy?
Part of me wants to think that you would have,
but the darker truth haunts me:
You would have thrown me out of your house.
There's no way that your boy could do those things,
even though your boy would do things with your
best friend after your passing, after he married Mama,
becoming my stepdad. I'm sparing you the details, Daddy;
it's pointless sharing them now.

iv.

One of my fondest memories of you:
coming out of the bathroom after you showered,
bath towel around your waist,
vinyl spinning on the record player.
I don't remember what it was, perhaps jazz,
or blues, but it was funky enough for you
to dance. J and I were shocked and
broke into laughter as you
performed your Daddy show for us.

v.

I forgive you now. I can. You have long been gone,
but what keeps you close to me is
your absence. It's fine. I get it now. I am a grown ass Man.
Tethered is never the way to live, right?
Daddy, you come and go as you please. Do whatever the
fuck you want, never questioned. I understand
because I am your little boy. Whether you would have
rejected me or not, I am your son. It doesn't matter.
I'm already abandoned, been that way for decades,
just wondering what you would have said.

vi.

Mama never stopped loving you. Even though
you were a slut, just like me. But the difference is,
I can't get men pregnant. She knew what she was
getting into and stepped into her role:
the beautiful wife of the big fish in the small pond.
I've seen the pictures. You both lived the life in that small
town. For years you owned the club that was the spot
before burning it down for the insurance money.
You and Mama always impeccably turned out,
dancing in cocktail dresses and fine suits.
Just such bad asses, couldn't tell you nothin'. You knew
what was going on always because you controlled everything.
Or, so you thought. We don't know we're not in control
until it's too late. Sometimes we do, if we are self-aware.
Were you self-aware, Daddy?
It's fine. It's OK. You also had a daddy who wanted to make
you into a Man, and he did. He most definitely did.

Mother

My first teacher, she
was the best one.
Beautiful, she floated
through a Tennessee county
as though she owned it,
as if a woman of her ilk
couldn't maintain in a town
the size of a pinprick, the
population of a petri dish.

I cannot explain her.

Words are recorded about what life

was like where I was born and raised.

In a place where Black boys are told:
You can't do that;

you have to behave.

*The woods around here get dark at night.
Things happen you really don't want
to know about but discover later.*

What Are You Doing?
for Jessie Wohlers

I am not planting a weeping willow in the backyard. I am just sitting here. Eating. I am knitting a sweater as I look distantly with sarcasm all over my face. I am cutting open the casing of sausages and putting them in a bowl. Filing my long almond-shaped acrylic nails before I put them on. I am making my shoes. I am gonna pull out one of my molars later. I just ordered a life-size Pikachu costume online. Tonight I'm gonna make a bronze cast of my cats' paws. I decided I'm going to get a grill … for my teeth. I've decided I'm going to become a calligraphist. **sigh** Peeing. I'm drawing on my eyebrows. I've decided I'm gonna buy all the googly eyes at Michaels if I win the lottery. Checking the Guinness World Records website to see who holds the world record for planking. Contemplating what Metta World Peace thinks about world peace. Memorizing every muscle in the human body. Staring at the wall. Ordering a katana blade online. Drawing up plans for our panic room. Researching the youngest person to ever get their teeth kicked out by a horse. Grazing. Trying to figure out how to transform this horse into a unicorn. Eating oysters on a half shell while humming the theme song to *Teenage Mutant Ninja Turtles*. Watching *The Real Housewives of Atlanta* while I wait for the Xanax to kick in. Deciding if I should become a cowboy or an equestrian. By the power of Grayskull, I have the power. Thundercats, hoooooooo!!

Remembering Samantha Fox

Naughty girls need love too
Naughty girls love to need
Naughty need to love girls
Naughty love needs to girls

Love needs girl naughty too
Love naughty girls to need
Love to girls need naughty
Love needs naughty to girls

Girls need naughty love too
To girl naughty love need
Girl naughty need to love
Girls love to need naughty

Need naughty girls love too
Need love to naughty girls
Two need girls naughty love
Need girls to love naughty

Two girls need naughty love
Too naughty need love girls
To love girl naughty need
To need girl love naughty

Boys love naughty girls
Naughty boys need love too
Naughty boys need naughty girls to love
Without naughty need there is no love too

Manhattan

With a modicum of grace,
a smidge of integrity and intelligence,

we move through this place like
bumper cars, banging into walls,

each other, clack clash of voices,
screams, and throated violence.

The niceness is cutting,
cordial, but with an edge,

or telling someone's Mama.
People are people,

even when they are being inhuman.

This city can bring out the beast
in the best of us,

knocking down skyscrapers,
eating homeless people for lunch.

Three Wishes

Rub the genie of the lamp
the right way, and he
will grant you three wishes:

*

A fertile body garden,
full of plump ripe limbs,
longing to be touched, plucked.

*

A son of a vision,
he will be my pride and joy,
my liquid message spilled from heaven.

*

A rain dance,
including thunder and lightning,
that leaves me waterlogged.

Three Wishes II

*Rub the genie of the lamp
the wrong way, and he will
take three things away from you:*

    *

Your name

    *

Your father

    *

Your promise

Anti-War Haiku

    1.
Forget the look of
the body as you know it.
War disfigures us.

    2.
My sex is honest.
His is a thick mushroom cloud,
strokes nuclear heads.

    3.
City streets fill with
the crunch of human traffic
ducking for cover.

    4.
Go slow, the day is
war-torn. Scraps float in the air,
softly suffocate.

    5.
Survive. Survive it.
Gather yourself in the wake.
The body is not.

S/M

Secular/Modernism

Scholastic/Manipulation

Sloppy/Meltdown

Satin/Malignancy

Savior/Misfit

Stale/Memento

Saintly/Masochistic

Supine/Mister

Sensual/Malediction

Salty/Marrow

Subtle/Minstrelsy

Sperm/Mess

Sassy/Monster

Shady/Marriage

Shaft/Magnet

Sadist/Memorabilia

Sweetly/Manhandled

Sex/Malfunction

Suddenly/Metaphysical

Shish kebab/Meat

Clothes/Whore

Cashmere.
I want to dress my tongue in it.
Let the soft, fuzzy fur coat my mouth.

Maybe my distraction is tight jeans
and little T-shirts that show off the physique.
Sometimes I like zip-up sweaters;
other times, I enjoy the convenience
of a pullover.

I pull him under.

Let's not even get into shoes;
we'll be here all day (and night),
which I'm not wholly against, but I
feel we could talk about other things.

Such as fabrics.
Silk, for instance, should be hand-washed,
loved, and worn sparingly.

I should wear this man sparingly,
instead of exhausting him all at once.

I like button-down shirts.

I appreciate clothes, but I prefer them
on something else, like mannequins,
or the floor, someplace different where they
may be admired.

What about houndstooth?
Or seersucker suits?
But does it always have to be about patterns?

Fucking DJ

So, the night is summer warm.
We, a constant hot mess,
stumble to his Tribeca flat.
Cars pass on Broadway.
We are at full mast.
He is a luxury that I do not always
get to know. We've been doing it for
a while. On our way here, he has already
blown me in a dark stairwell beneath
the street. Oh well, when you got to
you got to. He, of course, invites me
to the roof. I say "yes."
We go in and ride the elevator
past his sleeping fiancée.
The fiancée. She is a
woman who does not know
her man at all. She does
not know that he dreams of me
daily and is experiencing
me now in piping hot flesh.
His prayers answered.
As we ascend, the voices of my
friends begin in my head,
"He's engaged."
"What are you doing?"
"This is wrong."
My stock answer, of course:
"Well, if it's not me, it's going to be someone else."

And then I'm absolved.
We reach the roof.
A warm garden of fauna and lust
and the view.
We kiss until our tongues fall down
each other's throats. He begins.
Two buttons and two zips.
Prophylactic.
He sits in my lap
And we gaze down
toward the lower Manhattan skyline.

City Streets

—*Nobody is saying it's your fault, Arthur!*

I overheard a woman say on my way to the subway.
I looked to see a family of four standing on the corner
of 8th Ave. and 34th St. They are clearly tourists, and
they are clearly lost. I consider helping them out, showing
them that New Yorkers can be nice, kind, helpful people.
I decide against that, of course, because really, I can't
be bothered, especially by tourists. Who has the time?!

I continue down into the subway and head back to Brooklyn.
You hardly see tourists there, thank God, not even in
Prospect Park. They are all in Central Park getting their rocks
off taking pictures of Strawberry Fields or the fucking reservoir.
I used to go to the Rambles when I lived uptown in Harlem.
Best cruising in the city!! Far removed from the more popular
parts of the park, men are fruit dangling from trees, ripe for the
picking. Nothing beats outdoor sex. There's something very primal
about it: it's just you, a stranger (no names exchanged, that would
ruin the experience), and nature. It's how God fucking intended!
The Rambles is notorious for gay sex; I don't think I ever saw
any tourists there.

On the train back to the BK these two women are gossiping
about a friend:

—*Well, you should have seen her all over Beth's friend Cam
at this party. She was shameless!*

—Ugh, she's such a slut.

I wonder if my friends talk about me like that. I'm pretty open about my sluttiness, so it's common knowledge, not something that any of them would salaciously discuss on the L train; and considering the things they've said to my face, I figure what they're saying behind my back is really nothing to worry my pretty little head over.

On Seeing Richter

When the universe is
not coloring, then it must
be thinking about colors,
or what to make of blank
spaces that linger past
galaxies.

In this cityscape
at the MoMA,
there are black and gray
textures layered on top of
one another.
Smoky angles
billowing off canvas
street corners, sidewalks
busy with strokes.
People wait for colors.
Some shred of red that
might liven up their lives,
blue notes,
golden rays of shine.

Right now, we
have some nature. It wraps us up
in its warmness, lets us absorb
until nothing is left but gray.
Or it punishes and reminds us.
It gives and we take for granted all
that is beautiful and available for
our eyes.

One day we will see nothing,
and then what?

Whore/Genius

I'm looking for a transaction.
Yeah, ya know, something
to pique my ears, perk my
interest. What are you looking for?
A savant? Someone who
knows how to navigate the body
like an elegant puzzle?

How far do I cast?
Well, you can't afford
this shade, actually; I'm
too stark for you, too much
minimalist, too much
Mensa.

I'm too heady to even think
that far ahead. Which hotel?
How do we get there?
How quickly can you solve
this differential equation?
Are you good at mazes?

Love Poem #3

Read this from the side,
or if you prefer,
you may flip it over
and read this from the back.

Now that you've read this
from the back (or the side,
whichever you desire),
turn it over,
place it on top of you,
and read here from below.
Maybe it is not the one,
but it sure does feel like it.

Since you've read this
from below, place it on its back,
climb on top, and read this
from above.
Look down and tell it
you are not ready for it to end.

Grindr Vibin'

This Is Like Window Shopping for Dicks

Very horny cocksucker here.
Here for kicks. I am on a hunk hunt. Brooklyn,
ya dig? Most of you terrify me. I hope you step
on a Lego in the dark.

I'm Not Cis/Don't Be Rude

You can live your life or mine, but you can't
live both. Free your mind, and your ass will follow.
Anybody can take off his clothes, but can a bitch
hold a decent conversation?

Ask Him to Tell You More about Himself

I want to be so ugly I'm
beautiful; let me do the splits on your face. Am I the only
hopeless Romantic left? Ask away …

Do You Want to Get High off My Love?

Just like you, I get horny too.
Boulders of black diamonds, carved with bows,
saws, metal teeth, and blasts of human breath await.
Inhale the terms of this service; your name is alive now.

Sizing Him Up

He speaks and says things
that I don't hear.
Words drop to the floor
and shatter.
I kick the pieces to the side.
Heads nod.
If he knew the images running
through my mind, he would hit me.
That would bring me pleasure too.
I just want a touch,
a sign to let me know that I exist
beyond existence.

He speaks and says things
that I swallow.
Words churn, digesting.
I will let them go later
and forget what has passed through me.
If he knew of the restraint tying me up,
he would make the knots tighter,
kill my breath.
I just want to touch
a sigh of release,
knowing existence.

Same-Sex Coupling

    &
I don't want to be a hooker on the run.
People are constantly after you.
They put your name in their mouths

    &
spit it out fractured, fiery.
I want to move around in elegant tension
with a man who knows how to pluck

    &
plunder with the best of them,
a caged beast released to play,
a caveat presented at the right time.

Destruction/Desire

I'm your wrecking ball,
tearing you down to your foundation.
We must first verify our righteous intimacies
before we may consecrate them.
Just in case you didn't know,
I'm going to split you in half
like a coconut and take the milk for myself.
In the aftermath, we must be ready
to receive elements of the sublime.
Giving into your first impulse
is a sign of greatness, a signifier
of one's confidence.
I'm not going to break your heart,
just mutilate it a little: micro abrasions,
tiny cuts, maybe a cigarette burn or two.
But my lips, lichen on your limbs,
leave you incapacitated,
and then you are ended.

I Go Around Collecting Men

On Manhattan streets lit like Christmas,
the avenue gives night on a
plate.

This time in an adult bookstore,
a glance, a hand. This breath
is his. I am the one in anger.

Outside, there is a fuck across the street
in the truck. He rolls down his window
gives a grin. An avenue is crossed.

Consent

It is very simple:

Yes.

Mmmm   hmmm.

Just like that.

Keep going.

Take me to that
place where I
don't know where
I am.

Oh yeah.

Fuck.

Yes.

Don't stop.
Keep going.

Oh yeah

Yes Yes Yes

Mmmhmm
Mmmhmm
Mmmhmm

love poem #9

i lost him in the folds of the sheets.
and was left to finish the job myself.
not the first time. won't be the last.
i used to do this to make myself feel
bad. nothing better than cuddling with
a wad of guilt before falling asleep. now
i feel okay. relaxed. in this mess
lies every fantasy i have had.
glaring bare-eyed at the sun. leaving
my mark on cute boys. finding true love.
going to disneyland. and other
sadomasochistic things. nocturnal emissions
don't count. cleaning it all up is always the best part.
sanitize. put them away until next time.
maybe. just maybe. i will never need
them again. now. i have gone missing.

I Should Have Been a Gay Porn Star
for Donald Trump

I should have taken to the Valley
and started a new life as a versatile
fucker. I look okay naked. I've definitely
seen worse in porn both gay and straight;
for example, Ron Jeremy: I mean, really?
You would watch me in all the categories:
daddy videos, muscle hunks,
big Black cocks, twinks, Latin poppies, and so on.
I last way longer than they do without the Viagra
or the fluffers, because I'm just that good.
I'd lie to my family about how I'm making my fortune,
tell them that I work in real estate, even though I've
never been good with money.

I'd have porn star boyfriends with hot bodies and
big dicks. We'd fuck until we were bored with each
other and move on. The drugs and alcohol would flow
whenever I wanted, because who gives a fuck? I'm a
fucking porn star. Maybe my friends would be superficial
and vapid, only hanging out with me because of my
fortune and hedonistic fame, but it's LA!
It's OK because I just want people surrounding me,
basking in my pornographic glow. I'd probably do
what every porn star wants and cross over to
legit films and become Hollywood famous.
Or maybe my life would turn into *Boogie Nights*,
but the gay version. Instead of "Roller Girl,"
there's "Roller Guy." We fall in love
and fuck off into the sunset.

J/K

Just/Kindred

Jargon/Kisser

Joke/King

Jeopardy/Know

Jaw/Knuckles

Justice/Kidding

Job/Kicks

Jet/Kite

Jingle/Key

Jackal/Kitty

Jammed/Knot

Jeweled/Keepsake

Jester/Knight

Jar/Ketchup

Jealous/Knitter

Juice/Kale

Jihad/Killer

Jail/Keeps

American Logic

They say that here, you can do anything. So they say. You can come here and sweat, if you want. Dreams are made of what you conquered that day, things you plundered and whatnot. You have to know what you want; otherwise, you will be pushed to the side, marginalized maybe, thinking about how you can squeeze your way in without being detained. At this moment, however, a virus rages like hurricanes in a warm ocean; it overtakes bodies and declares them colonized, mostly bodies of color, of course, because that's the way it goes; the irrational is rational, is spreading disease and poverty among its most vulnerable. In America, we vote in our worst interests; we punish the poor. We love the things that destroy us. We have to have everything that others do not. So fulfilling. We want to be filled with all the materials, grace, and admiration that Jesus will allow us. If you don't believe in Jesus, you are problematic. Everyone must believe in God, but you must also believe in Jesus and how he lived. We don't live as Jesus lived. We laud his life as aspirational yet continue to shit on others. Oh well, what are you going to do? It's not my fault. I did the best I could. This isn't my problem. It's yours. Maybe someday those people will learn.

Love Poem #15

Single Black male
in search of
a single male
who enjoys
being splayed out
on a page.
Intimate details
not necessary.
Must like
nothing,
maybe himself,
but I'm easy.
Must be skin,
and hair, and scent.
No preference regarding
trifling things like skin color,
height, or weight,
but flexibility is required.
If interested, reply to men
you see on the streets.

The Milky Way

On a bed of clustered stars,
I lie my head down on the moon.
I close my eyes and think
about the elegance of scars:

that rusty nail, rug burn, rope burn, welts
and cuts. My body is a decaying temple,
a tenement building,
an unfinished book marked by stars.

Appreciation

Appreciate that you don't have children.

Even during these days, you wake up, look outside your Brooklyn window.
It is raining.

The planet spins on its axis, wobbles a bit. It is quieter now.

You should appreciate that time is nothing anymore.

You are safe, taken care of.

The books have always been neatly stacked on the floor.
Still can't choose a bookcase.

The bed seduces you again.

"The life of Riley" is what Grandpa always said. The hills he walked in snow.

You should appreciate the fact that you go around collecting people. At least, you used to out on those streets coerced into being yours. You don't even remember how you did it.

Owned by your body and not someone else's.

Pace and sigh. You'll get out of here someday.

Acknowledgments

Thank you to the journals, magazines, and anthologies that have published versions of these poems:

The Brooklyn Rail: "Clothes/Whore"
Obsidian: "Whore/Genius," "Poet/Manifesto," "I Go Around Collecting Men," "Heartbreaker," "Mother"
A Gathering of the Tribes: "Appreciation," "Through the Window"
Flicker and Spark: A Contemporary Queer Anthology: "Fucking D.J." "S/M," "Anti-War Haiku"
Ostrich Review: "Grindr Vibin'"
Poetry is Bread Anthology: "What Are You Doing?"
Vanderbilt Review: "Possum Feet," "My Father's Shoes"

Much gratitude to Cave Canem and the community of Black poets that I am so honored to be a part of. This book would not exist without the support from so many talented, gifted people in this fellowship.

Many of these poems were generated and/or workshopped at the Community of Writers retreat and the Colgate Writers Conference. Thank you for your valuable feedback and all the friendships we made.

I have so much love and gratitude to so many people in my life who I am fortunate to call family, both blood related and chosen:

Thank you to the still not officially named collective that is Sheila Maldonado (thank you for naming this book), David Pemberton, Stella Padnos, Mike Ptaszek, David Aglow, and Erika Jo Brown.

Thank you to the brilliant Krista Franklin for the beautiful and unique cover art for this collection and for your friendship and love.

Thank you to Gabriel García Román for making me a Queer Icon and for being one yourself.

Much love to Rosebud, Robin, Michelle, Cheri, and Tonya.

Thank you to Mark Jarman, Wayne Koestenbaum, Ronaldo Wilson, and Margot Douaihy for your kind and gracious blurbs for this collection.

Thank you to the Bad Trinity (Bergen and Jeremiah), Tina, Esti, Shannon, Pierre, and Scott for your support, unconditional love, and friendship.

Thank you to Nicole, Will, Robin, Martha, Bradley, and Ronit for your years of friendship.

Thank you to Cornelia and Carrie for the supportive phone calls through the years. We'll always have Nashville.

Thank you to my therapist, Martine. This book would not have happened if it were not for your insights and the work we did together over the years. I am forever grateful and humbled.

Thank you to Roberto Garcia and everyone at Get Fresh Books for taking on this project.

Thank you to my family, in particular: my brother Jerry Wilson, Jr., my niece Zoe, my cousins Misty and Crystal, and my Aunt Gwen & Aunt Hope; thank you to my Uncle Terry and Aunt Joanne. I love y'all so very much!

Author Bio

Bakar Wilson has received fellowships from Cave Canem, the Community of Writers, and the Colgate Writers' Conference. He has performed his work at the Bowery Poetry Club, Poetry Project, The Studio Museum of Harlem, and the Asian-American Writer's Workshop among others. His poetry has appeared in *The Vanderbilt Review*, The *Lumberyard Radio Magazine*, *The Brooklyn Rail*, *Flicker and Spark: A Contemporary Queer Anthology*, *The Ostrich Review*, and *Obsidian Magazine* among others. Wilson curated and hosted an hour of poetry at the Whitney Biennial in 2022 for their poetry marathon in collaboration with A Gathering of the Tribes and received a commission from the Metropolitan Museum of Art in 2022 for Juneteenth. A native of Memphis, Tennessee, Wilson received his B.A. in English from Vanderbilt University and his M.A. in Creative Writing from the City College of New York. He lives in Brooklyn, NY.

www.ingramcontent.com/pod-product-compliance
Lightning Source LLC
LaVergne TN
LVHW081456060526
838201LV00051BA/1813